I0441542

Oh My God:
Black People Are Cruel To Each Other

Hollywood Set Me Up To Take The Fall:
Blacks Murdered Me!

By

Angela C. Williams

ISBN-13: 9781515274698
ISBN-10: 1515274691

Angela C. Williams

Table of Contents

Introduction

My School-Aged Years

I haven't always been homeless. In fact I lived a great childhood and my early adult life started out plush and very eventful. One might say I felt very lucky; blessed even. It was a neighborhood with two entrances. Neither had a sign that let a driver know that they had arrived. You were now in Ritchie Manor off of Ritchie Road; where the children went to Ritchie Elementary and in my home, they lived on Richville Drive and watched the cartoon, Richie Rich. Our house was small but it had 4 bedrooms and 1 ½ bathrooms. No dishwasher, no fireplace and no pantry. I can only speak for our household when I say. We weren't rich, but we didn't want for anything. Oh, and did I tell you that Woody Wood Pecker lived behind my house? ("No"). Well, he did.

Our neighborhood was full of young kids who enjoyed playing together. My house was in the back of the neighborhood on the last street. Our house was in the middle of our street. There was no house directly across from us so when we hosted our large family for cook-outs, there was always somewhere to park. The location of our home was great for kick-ball and dodge ball. The sidewalk was perfect for double- dutch and roller skating. There was only one thing we had to worry about. The neighborhood terror. This new family moved in two doors down and brought this frightening German Shepard. You would think that they would have purchased a thicker chain or a taller fence. For ten years, he popped his chain and chased the nearest person into a frenzy. He actually bit a few people. You wanna know his name? He has the same name as the toy doll who comes to life and stabs his victims to death. He has the same name as the big mouse with the pizza adventure land for, children's birthdays.

We had a dog for a little while when I was 5. He used to pop his chain too but he didn't bite people. Eventually, he ran away. I guess looking back, they were both scared of the animals in the woods behind our homes.

My mother always had birthday parties for me and my brother. It's warm during my birthday and it falls near a holiday and sometimes Spring Break. We would usually not have trouble getting the entire family to come to a cook-out during a holiday; and even our numerous family friends.

My mother used to manage a bank and believe it or not she used to take me to work with her when I was really little; I remember. She was good friends with a lady from India. She shared the name of the puppy on the cartoon Arthur. It was really fun. She eventually left to work for the postal service, like my father. He's worked the night shift ever since I could remember. My mother worked her way up to supervisor but he chose to keep his position and shift. I'm saddened when I think that neither me nor my brother were in a position to take care of our parents the way they took care of us. But at least they had each other after we left.

Although my mom was not a haunted Plymouth vehicle, she drove very fast. That is her name. Christine, like the movie. She called her bosses, Boss and she was married to a mouse whom she could never catch, in a silent cartoon. Yes that's my dad's name. Well it's just like the ocean…under the moon…; no my brother is not a Spanish singer but he shares his first name. (Give us your heart, make it real or just forget about it).

Our parents worked hard but they played hard too. They loved to travel. When we were young, they took us everywhere. We had a conversion van that allowed us to take road trips in comfort, before gas prices were high and unstable. When we were very young, we flew once and drove down a few years later, to Sea World and Disney World in Orlando, Florida. After my mother's brother was relocated to Wisconsin by his employer, we drove way up there to visit. When I was ten and my brother was sixteen, we drove in a caravan with two other families from the neighborhood, to the World's Fair in New Orleans, Louisiana. Our male cousin who share the name of the son on *The Fresh Prince*, went with us. Everybody had a riding partner. My father or brother rode with me. I forgot to tell you why I couldn't get in the pool at the hotel. A week or so before our trip, I was riding my ten speed with the girl who invited me to play basketball, on the back of my bike. We got up our speed so that when we passed the house with the big dog, we would just sail on by. I didn't work out that way. He was in the front and his bark scared me so much that I crashed my bike. She walked home and I walked my bike home. Bloody and scarred, (obviously discombobulated), I tucked myself into bed. My brother was in his room and my dad was downstairs watching TV. When my mom got home she came in my room and I was bloody and scarred. She yelled at both of them. I couldn't remember where we fell; she asked me. We had to go get my friend and she told my mom what happened. (I didn't have restrictions as to where I could ride within the neighborhood. I wasn't lying. I truly didn't remember). I'm not a doctor so I didn't know that I needed x-rays and a scan of my brain. I had stitches and a big giant bandage on my side. My mom keep it clean and changed my bandage regularly but my trip was not quite as fun as it probably could have been. But it's OK because my brother and I had a lot of stuff around the house to keep us busy. We played cars, Battleship, Connect Four and even had out own arcade sized pinball machine. Every Friday our parents bought dinner from a different carry-out and sometimes we would play Bingo, Monopoly or Scrabble. Speaking of stiches; my former friend, the surgeon; sister of the anesthesiologist, used to play dolls and house with me and the girls in my neighborhood. Me, her and another little girl, were lying on the ground pretending to be in bed and I needed more space, so I told her to roll-over. She fell down from ground level to the bottom of the basement steps, right in front of the basement door. She busted her chin. We had to rush her to the emergency room. You would think that experience led her to become a doctor but not quite.

Two of my mother's female friend's had a devastating health issue at a much younger age. Fortunately, they survived. The mother of these two previously mentioned doctors, had an aneurism. The mother of the young woman whose first name is my middle name; had breast cancer. They are both still alive and well.

A few years later, for a couple of weeks during the summer, my mom and dad sent me and my brother (alone on a plane) to visit her other brother and his family in Melbourne, Florida. Although he lived in Greece many years before he was stationed in Melbourne, we didn't fly overseas as a family to visit.

I ended up going to Europe in the 9thgrade with the French Club. I was taking Spanish, but it was an opportunity that I didn't want to miss. I celebrated my 15th birthday in Europe. It was great. I've never been attacked by a bidet-(*BAPS*). I've never fallen in love with one either- (*Jumping the Broom*). I'd never seen one and I used it once when we first got there. My super fantastic moment of celebration can actually be matched by a super scary moment when I left my purse on the train; in (I believe it was), Switzerland. As I exited the train, I realized my purse was not with me. It had my traveler's checks inside. I don't remember if our chaperone held on to all of our passports or not, but I ran back down the platform and onto the train. I was frantic hoping that the train didn't pull off. I grabbed my purse and rejoined my group. In hind-sight I guess being separated from my group and lost in another country would have been much worse than replacing my traveler's checks.

One day my mother came home from work around 4:30 in the evening and it was pouring down raining. I met her at the door with a towel. I can no longer make it through the day at work. I'm still dancing around the house. I hope she knows that I'm doing the best that I can. My parents never really argued but my brother left. Leaving gave him a second chance. I cry every time I hear the song.

Both sides of my family has always had family reunions on a fairly regular basis. My father's side more frequently than my mom. I don't know which is true. My mother's side of the family stopped having reunions after my mom passed away or after my younger female cousins got married. I think they are all keeping their men locked away for safe keeping.

My father's, mother's, brother's, wife (or his aunt, through marriage) is still living and we are still in touch with that extended family. Meet them. May I introduce them? I only eat the Brown M&M's cause chocolates already Brown. They are very nice and they are all very accomplished. (Mind you; that is the last name of the young lady whose birthday is on September 11th; and my grandmother's maiden name). Our reunion is always the weekend of my grandmother's birthday. I guess I'll see them this fall. Here's the catch. My only nephew graduates from high school this spring near Tampa. If I ride down there with my dad and stay so that I can move to Miami near my brother I won't make it to my grandson's first family reunion. Who will watch my grandson?

When I was in elementary school, my father's dad was found dead on the sidewalk out-side of his home. He had apparently fallen or been thrown from his high-rise apartment window. I've never read the police report, however I wouldn't be surprised to find conflicting evidence. Could the movies, Beverly Hills Cop and I Robot be eluding to the need for a new investigation.

If you are a parent; whether you're obese or not, and you over heard your fifth grader on the phone talking about her boyfriend, would you be devastated. If you had a fifth grader who ate twice as much food during each meal, as your other children; would you be concerned. What if he or she didn't eat vegetables? What about smoking cigarettes or drinking alcohol? Are either of these reasons to stop either child from participating in extracurricular activities? You may not stop them but you definitely need to encourage them. Please keep in mind as you read; I do not have any addictions, nor have I ever. I've never smoked anything or abused alcohol or drugs.

I was invited to go to basketball practice with a friend of mine from the neighborhood when I was 9 years old. (A friend who shares the same last name as the scary family who named their daughter Wednesday). From that day forward I was hooked on the game. (Or maybe I was hooked on all the new friends and fun I was now having). Every season I played a sport with the community Boys and Girls Club. When football time rolled around; I cheered. I played basketball in the winter and softball in the summer. A lot of times, my mother, carpooled a lot of us to practice. We were really good. We had two coaches and one of them was, my (former) best friend and team-mates; father. Our other coach was an older white man who owned a property in Ocean City. Every summer he took three of us to the beach for a weekend. Including our other coach's daughter of course. Life was fun. I only wished I had encouraged my brother to get involved in Boys and Girls Club activities. I wonder why no young men invited him. I wonder what prompted her to invite me.

My mom took us to see Ice Capades every time they came into town.

My mother was like the team mom. She even got an award for being so dedicated to our team; during boys and girls club and high school. My dad worked at night so he missed all of my High school basketball games. The year I ran track; he traveled with us everywhere.

My mom loved to shop. I remember keeping a calendar on my wall logging every outfit; being sure not to wear anything twice in one month during high school. Even when I was smaller I was particular about my outfits. I recall walking through a department store with my mom wearing my all purple outfit to match my newly painted bedroom. (I asked if they could paint my room purple). I was walking with her and she said, "Where is your other shoe?" I said, "It's back there stuck in the escalator." My new purple Jordache sneaker. We went back to get it. I believe I was in the fourth grade.

I remember in elementary school when my mother bought her first dream car. She and my brother picked me up from 6th grade, in a really nice, brand-new, BMW. Unfortunately, my dad totaled it. (Not before my former friend, the Anesthesiologist, used it for her high school prom. But the important thing is that he is OK. His rib broke and punctured his lung. (The actor/actress is driving my mother's car in the movie Machete).

I remember my mother dropping me and my life-long neighbor and friend, (the spice from Gilligan's Island), at bible study on some Sundays. She and I played Barbie dream house in our basements on numerous occasions. We got our first ten-speed bikes on the same Christmas.

The dark side of my basement will always be like the dark side of the moon to me. (…..nothing to do with Mulan). I could never reach my arm around and turn on the light for fear that the monster would get my arm. So I would always fall to sleep on the couch and my brother would come downstairs, pick me up, put me in the bed and tuck me in.

I was taking a lot of dance classes at a small Fashion Institute that was preparing me to compete in the MISS TEEN Pageant; where I won 1st runner up; I was 14. Having the support of an entire community of friends, family and my parents' co-workers, was an awesome feeling. It almost felt surreal, being on stage with that many people clapping for you. (Angelica from the movie; *Six Days, Seven Nights;* my talent: my dance and my out-fit). Well, my hips aren't narrow anymore and my breast may actually be big enough now, too bad I don't look like her. Maybe I could have snagged my green-eyed friend from Wild World Amusement Park.

Oh yeah. That was my first job ever. I met a lot of people. Including my first love. I saw him and wanted to meet him. I was introduced and as I glanced at the other guys in the landscaping department, I immediately became overtaken by another guy. This green-eyed hunk. But it was too late. I composed myself and began a great love affair with the guy who was just as excited to meet me. Guess what happened. My new boyfriend, offered me a ride home. Great! Not great. The gorgeous hunk, was his best friend. He was riding home with us. No I didn't cheat. He was an OK boyfriend. Our mothers talked to one-another and everything. During the summer, he took me to the movies and a few times we returned to work on our day off, to enjoy the fun of the amusement park. Our mother's visited with each other and everything.

He even came to my first dance in high school. I don't remember him inviting me to any of his dances. Our relationship was strained because he didn't attend the same school as I did. Everyone was telling me that he had cheated on me with a girl at his school. They told me her name and everything. I think he must have been just flirting with her. (Oh, a plan to break us up-*High School Musical*). When I wasn't in school I was busy with sports. He was busy in the spring with baseball. They both played for their school. Something in my heart felt different. (Maybe he was mad because he was really overdressed at the Back-To-School Dance). I didn't know he was going to be all dressed up. He never invited me to go out anymore. After a year or so he and I broke up but we were still friends. I had a few other boyfriends during high school. Those relationships didn't last very long. I'm not sure what was said. We talked for a while once and I'm sure we entertained getting back together. But me and my first love ended up 'breaking up for good', (on the phone), right before the prom. I didn't cheat on him or anyone else. (Might not make sense to you, but it's the world of teen-agers). I decided that we shouldn't go to the prom together. I ended up going alone.

{He led the Redskins to victory in Super Bowl 22. (Just say his name over and over out loud to yourself). I had not long before, had sex for the first time in my life, with my boyfriend-(my first love). But my father sure watches a lot of sports on TV. He could probably draw out some plays. He even looks a little like him}. OMG. So this is the other reason why my high school coach gave me his daughter's jersey number; 22?

For the next year or so, I became closer friends with my ex's best friend. We talked on the phone. It was a while before I actually went over to his home. I think it all started when I found myself talking to him about being mad at my boyfriend years ago when he made me mad.

On prom night, I went to dinner at a restaurant on the water, with a group of friends, (other couples); before the Prom. Guess who I danced with during the first slow song? My Physics teacher. I thought I looked great and I felt beautiful. It was a great night. I went to a Prom after party at a hotel. It wasn't really my scene so I didn't stay long. Then I went to my green-eyed friend's house so he could see how pretty I looked. We slept on the basement floor in front of the TV; fully clothed, all nite; he snuck me in. No we didn't touch. The next morning I went home changed my clothes and went to Kings Dominion with the same group of friends of which I'd gone to the pre-Prom dinner.

Well, he moved to Florida and opened a Fitness Gym. Did I mention that the one and only time he came to my house, when high school was ending; he brought me a roll of cookie dough. He walked in, handed it to me and walked right back out? Yes I knew and still know how to make cookies in the oven, the proper way; I don't need Ingrid from Uptown Girls, to show me. *Clueless*. They're both married; and have been for some time now. Well, anyway....Maybe I'll see him and his family when I go visit my brother. Maybe I won't. Maybe I'll run into my ex when I'm 50, and he'll be single; I doubt it because the last time I ran into him, he was really rude. I'm not sure why. When I ran into him while pan-handling a few years back he came to my hotel and played scrabble with me. Back to b-ball with my girls:

When it was time for high school, many of us were used to playing ball together so we won a lot of games even though we were short. We made it to the State Championship all four years. We made it; but we came in second every time. (Our coach always said "No one ever remembers who comes in second"). *Welcome Home Roscoe Jenkins*. I don't know what they feed those Broadneck girls; they were all ginormous!

I recall my girlfriend's, sister's boyfriend moving to Colorado. She shares the name of the daughter of the 42nd President. He was in the Air Force and that was where he was stationed. She decided to attend college out there to be near him. Me and my girlfriend flew out to visit her sister during our spring-break. Colorado is absolutely breath-taking. And although her relationship didn't work out and she had a baby before she finished college, she completed medical school on the East-Coast and is now an Anesthesiologist. You go girl!

My mother's friend worked for an entertainment company and was able to get her tickets to some major concerts. During the last two years of high school, during college and a few years after college; me and my mom, were blessed enough to get great seats to the concerts of, Janet Jackson, Michael Jackson and Maxwell. My mother and I went to see Michael but I was able to invite a friend to go with me to see the other artists.

Even though I didn't accept the basketball scholarship to Salisbury, I played intramural basketball at Towson, for fun and exercise. Ok, I should have known to join a media club of some sort even if I wasn't guided to do so. I guess I hadn't really decided what part of Mass Comm I'd desired to work. I remember speaking with my green-eyed friend who was attending Hampton. He shared with me that he would be transferring to another college because his current school did not have his particular major.

I decided to join a Christian Sorority called ANQ. I recall driving down to Atlanta, Georgia to a Christian Conference with 3 of my frat brothers and 3 of my sorors. There was a snow storm brewing, but we'd already paid our money so we took our time and took turns driving the minivan we'd rented. I was friends with a lot of male and female freshmen on campus. But the new, third-string, freshman quarterback introduced me to my husband. He said we sounded a lot alike when it came to the things of God. No I did not allow him to spend the night. We spent the majority of our time hanging out in my apartment and working out on the track. My soon to be husband, was too busy anyway. He was in and out of town and focused on trying to become a pro-ball player. He was a cornerback. He left school, before graduating to play on the Redskins practice squad. He only had 11 credits to go but that was a chance of a life-time. His jersey number was 22. My jersey number was 22.

During this period, my parents were traveling a lot. Long cruises to the cost of Mexico and other Islands; a trip to Alaska, a trip to Africa. And a train ride across country. Thanks *Home Alone* for the credits that may have led my mom to travel. Who knew she would get sick at such a young age.

Now during my relationship with my soon to be husband, I was very focused on graduating. He was traveling and trying to land a contract with the Redskins. I was wondering why I hadn't been invited to meet his mom and dad yet. Come to find out, his ex-girlfriend had fought with her mom and was staying at his mother's. (He lived there too). His parents didn't know for a long time that there was someone else. He called me from LA one night talking 'bout SHE was with him and she said she was pregnant. I cried for months. He had taken her to the Redskins cook-out while he was supposed to be with me. By the way, you know that girl who sucked the former president's penis; yeah, that was his ex-girlfriends name. (Is that what he wanted from me?) Come to find out, she wasn't pregnant and she left him when he got cut from the Redskins practice squad. He showed up a year later at my door, with flowers; in tears. Against my friends and family member's advice, I took him back. He didn't even have a job. I graduated and found a job as a Reprographics Assistant in the Graphics Department of an Architect firm. I told him that if we were going to continue having sex and he wanted to spend the night, we had to get married. But we planned our wedding. Three months later I was pregnant. I named my daughter after the character in *Mo' Better Blues*. (I was not pregnant when I got married). No, the movie wasn't about me and I've never been to Harlem, but I was dark skinned, and I'd won. It's so sad that things happened the way they did. I, (we), gave up on our marriage so soon. (I wish we'd traveled to an island or taken a cruise for our honeymoon). We went to the Poconos. Can you blame me for trying to form a solid marriage union at an early age?

The new Cinderella movie just came out last week. The light-skinned actor from Mo' Better Blues, shares my last name; in real-life. So I guess she is the real Cinderella. Cause I'm still single. Lol. Maybe I'm still single because an actor/actress whose name in real–life happens to be the same as mine, said in a movie called Waiting to Exhale; when asked about her failed marriage by a fellow actor, that she was not about to go out and find herself a new owner.

Speaking of failed marriage; I suppose the theme song, "Are you that special someone?", from Dr. Doolittle (1998) and the name Blossoms Mammoth Circus; has nothing to do with me being hurt by men who didn't take a relationship with me, seriously (After my divorce). I just noticed the Mammoth Circus scene at the end of the movie, today. May, 2015.

Back on campus:

It seemed as if those who didn't come to school with their best friends, became best friends with their room-mates. My room-mate was from my high-school but, unfortunately she didn't make the grades and lost her scholarship. She was smart but she became a sweetheart to a frat boy and the rest is history. She ended up leaving. She ended up at a larger University and has since graduated and is doing fine. My closest girlfriends had gone to school at Hampton and at MD Eastern Shore where there were a lot of guys from our area and our high school. I wonder if any of my friends ever fell sexually with any of them. I'm kind of surprised that it took them so long to find a life-mate and to have children.

I ended up with a nice White room-mate when I moved off campus. One of my sorors introduced us. She was barely home because she took a job as a nanny for a couple of young children in a neighboring county. I think I sort of pushed her away when I tried to minister to her one day. When she was home, her boyfriend from Bethany Beach was there too. A very attractive black guy. He spent the night quite often. That is not why I ministered to her though.

I remember my parents driving up to my gospel choir concert. It was really nice. My mom also drove up for my induction into the sorority. My pharmacist friend and her mom drove up for the induction as well.

My brother had sort of been coerced into enlisting in the military. He joined the Marines. I know he doesn't regret it. I remember going to his Graduation Ceremony in Parris Island, South Carolina. Soon after, he was stationed in Yuma, Arizona. He told me it was so hot there that you could see the heat rising from the ground. He might as well had been stationed in Africa!.... Well, not quite. You can't take a cross-country road trip home, from Africa. Can you believe he caught the bus home! (One day I hope to drive my daughter cross country to see the west coast). (According to her, she doesn't fly). He'd decided to get out of the military. He married shortly before me but we had our child shortly before them. Long story short, neither marriage worked out.

I was home, he was home, and my entire family came from miles around; crossed states even; to celebrate my daughters first birthday (It was my mother's sister's birthday too). My brother was the clown at her party. That was the theme. It was a cook-out. My daughter's father was there too. Unfortunately my husband didn't take the opportunity that posed itself, to try to rekindle our flame, other than attempting to sleep in the same bed with me. It was clearly over. Can you believe his mother called me talking bout' "he has needs". Not, He loves you and we should try to work it out by going on vacation; but, "he has needs". No, I did not have sex with him.

Now if you think that all of the situations with womanizers in college and the negative outcome with my marriage should make me aware of how volatile relationships with guys can be, you have to wonder why I only am able to have male friends after I return home from a failed marriage. A group of girlfriends rallying around me and helping me thrive again would have been very appropriate. Can't say I didn't try to make that happen.

Apparently, my brother couldn't find a permanent place to live (until he could get back on his feet). Not one family member. I don't remember saying he couldn't live with me and I had literally just gotten keys to my apartment. He and his wife had a son the same age as my daughter and they had recently broken up as well.

I know my brother's heart must have been broken and I feel bad. When a black male has one or two negative things happen in the early part of his life; he can definitely begin life with a defeated attitude. He left for Miami. He never moved back to this area. The tears of a clown-when no one's around. I might be cute but I ended up just being a substitute; deep inside I'm blue? Somebody's psychic, Lol.

Deep down in my gut I have a feeling that my brother's sabotage is worse than mine. He told me that he had his own place and a job when he first got there. (He lost his job and never got back on his feet, at least from the last I'd known. (Unfortunately he wasn't keeping in touch with me enough for me to know that his situation had become dire-years ago). It's probably because people are harassing him about his sister being a ho. Which I'm not. Recently, we spoke briefly. He has switched rolls with his girlfriend. She works while he stays at home. Sounds like my current life to a 'T'. Well, not to a 'T' cause I'm single. But my daughter thinks she's in the parent roll, because she's working and I'm not. (I'm watching her baby). I'm quite sure that no matter where my brother lived; Maryland or Florida; he would not have been able to pan-handle like I'm doing without being beaten by the cops. (Years ago-when I hadn't heard from him, I went looking for him). I'm a woman and I found myself toe to toe with men who carry guns, (cops); a few times. I guess he and I both are the designated homeless. It's funny because they all think we're jealous of them, (family and friends). Why would everyone be so mean to me and my brother?

I recall flying down to my uncles because we hadn't heard from my brother. I asked my uncle to drive me to Miami. I found my brother in a shelter. He drove back to Melbourne with us. I figured he would be OK from that day forward. By the time I got back home, I understand that he ended up back to Miami. I tried to help. I was living with my parents then. We have all really let my brother down. He was never a menace to society either. (Was I the one who'd found someone who didn't have anything and put em' off on family; family that now live in Newport?) – *Soul Food*. It is a relatively old movie. It would have to be some deep, deep sabotage to try to make scenes from **this movie**; come true. You and I both know, I would never be drinking to get drunk (I don't drink beer) and I would never go after someone else's husband; especially in their home. I don't drink beer. They wanted it to come true so badly, that their husband comes after me. Me and my daughter became homeless because I lost my job. You should never have forced me to move up there.

If I was the person they say. I would be rich from "ho-ing" or stripping. I am not a ho now, nor did I used to be. I just found out what "tricking" meant not too long ago.

OK I know he doesn't consider himself homeless anymore. He found love. I guess homelessness is a little different for military veterans. I hope so.

He loves his family. My brother was never violent in school or in our home. I've visited him several times and even tried to relocate once. I just didn't have the means or the money to do so. I love him. I truly miss him. I hope to live near him one day. He never joined any sports programs or joined any organizations in grade school but he is a very smart, kind person. I failed to mention that I cried all the way home after visiting him in 2004. I did not want to leave him.

Our Christmas' were grand. My mother was a giver. During the earlier part of the year, my brother used to always say something and then say sike. So one Christmas, I got a little box and wrapped it just for him. The only thing it contained was a note stating the word, sike. We all cracked up laughing. (His son sort of reminds you of the guy in the TV show Psyche). And the big brother's T-shirt has nothing but the word sike on the front in the movie- *Diary of a Wimpy Kid*. He and I got along for the most part. We definitely didn't fight like the two boys in this series of movies. Although he didn't used to be the best driver; that is definitely not him in Diary of a Wimpy Kid. He purchased a used old-timer car; you know the thick heavy kind. Unfortunately the brakes gave out and he ran into a police car. (Columbiana). That sounds like a very big ticket to me. If you can't pay your ticket they revoke your license. If you have no license, you have no job. I guess you have to use The mustang belonged to my neighbor who has the name of the spice from Gilligan's Island. I drove a Mercedes to the prom that did not belong to me. It belonged to a woman named Jackie.

I'm glad that my brother's son had such a fun and rewarding experience in grade school but it breaks my heart to know that my brother wasn't able to be a part of it. Anyone in a position to change his situation, should have. You can't get those precious moments back. Maybe they'll be closer now that his son is older and able to drive himself around.

I'm saddened to think that I can't get the time back that I've lost being so far away from my brother but I can only pray that we will see each other again and be able to enjoy each other's company for however long we have.

Some time ago I began a Small Business Management course at the local community college. I decided not to continue the class but forgot to drop the course. I simply walked away. I unknowingly acquired an 'E' on my transcript instead of what would have been an 'I' for Incomplete.

I took time to go back to graduate school in order to try to reboot myself. I chose a historically Black college to take my graduate level Education courses. Bowie state to be exact. I learned a lot but unfortunately the only class I really enjoyed was the class where the professor was White. But not before driving myself up to Columbia University to speak directly with an advisor about the Master of Journalism program. Although I never became a Broadcast Journalist, *Vantage Point* makes me sort of glad that I didn't. At least not somewhere dealing with political conflict. An actor/actress using my name is being blown-up while reporting. Maybe I can write stories for a newspaper or magazine, from 'home', Lol. I am now writing. I hope to write a few articles and books.

It's 1976 and I am 3 years old. The name of the Steakhouse has changed and our mother's were very close before mine passed away a little over 10 years ago. My middle name is her first name and our profiles are similar. I pray that neither one of our ships are sinking as on April 14, 1912. Although I'm the single parent, that's her mother's name. Her daughter is the one who is hard to impress in the movie Titanic. Is it September 11, 1792? Well, I'm not married. I hope she is.

I'm not feeling very lucky anymore, but I know I'm blessed.

Angela C. Williams

Black Lives Matter

I am a black woman, yet there's not a Black person I know who believes my life matters. I don't need to be a doctor to prove that I believe that everyone deserves a chance to make a better life for themselves and their children. I made a comment a few years ago that I couldn't be a doctor because I didn't think the 'Ho's lives were worth saving. I said it, to myself because I was mad because I'm being verbally harassed off of my jobs by dumbass Blacks. I'm also being called a ho and I know I'm not. I'm not ghetto either. I know that what I say is being heard by and repeated to many. Because of that comment, they now want me dead. I was left homeless with nothing to do for income but pan-handle. I suppose they believed I would sell my body. If you ask them, they will tell you that I did. But I never have. I'm not a ho but I'm 'labeled' no matter what.

My education hasn't really expired, I've just been battling those who don't want me to prosper. The sabotage began when I was small. They built it up slowly until it came tumbling down on top of me. Hollywood that is. I didn't know that I was supposed to stay in California near my cousin and all of this could have been avoided. I would have been spared the revelation that has exposed the Black race for the trifling, lazy, back-biting, self-centered, nut-jobs that they really are. I can dance and be full of joy in the midst of knowing that they all plan to shot me to death because I know I'm a child of God and I'm not a liar.

They don't want my life to matter so they all came together to concoct a plan to keep me from earning a living doing something that allows God to use me. In which of course, I would enjoy. Pleasing God makes me happy.

I don't even see how the millionaires in Hollywood sleep at night. If I obtained my life savings by murdering and destroying lives all over the world. I would not be proud of that.

A Community That Wants Me To Fail

I've lived here all of my life. I know a lot of people in a lot of career fields. They know of me and are well aware that I'm being slandered. Most were aware that I needed a foot I the door of my undergraduate career field but they chose to believe the lies from the TV and on the movie screen. Media swayed their decision in a negative direction. Yes they all knew that my marriage ended and that I was back home but they let the specifics of what they believed was my personal life, keep them from reaching out to me. Everyone was waiting for this to happen to me. The planned my death.

I volunteered in this community. I played sports in the Boys and Girls Club for years. My mother spent her spare time serving our team.

Black men had seen movies "about me" that I had yet to see. They figured, what the hell, I'm gonna dog her anyway. My female friends figured they'd just stop talking to me. They didn't' bother saying,"Have you seen that movie?" So ten years or so later I see the movies that caused me to lose all of my friends and all of my family.

They believe I'm a ho because they are whore-minded and not very bright. They want to make me believe that it makes sense to say that since I begged for 3 years out of the 6 that I was homeless that I shouldn't be able to use my brain to earn a living doing anything worth wild. These are the same people who left me homeless for no reason and verbally harassed off of each job acquired while homeless. So, how did they expect me to earn a living? Do you see my point? They have made themselves believe that I s_ck di_ks and have sex for money. Even knowing that I will probably be shot by a cop who believes the same lies, very soon; I am able to smile through my tears. I know God. I know the truth. Everyone kept saying "Go Home". But no one offered me a ride (to my father's), even when I asked.

No one would come and get their hair done.

Why not just ask a pan-handler to leave. Tell them next time you we'll call the police. Why try to get them arrested? Why send them before a judge?

Blacks are terrible people and they make the world a terrible place to live. They are now trying to pretend that inviting me to sell my books at church events as a vendor can somehow fix the problem of me being prospectively jailed for pan-handling or getting a warrant for running. Yes they waited until after I got charged to offer me what I'd been writing letters to them for, for years.

They all want me to die in jail, or be shot running. I haven't caused anyone's pain. They've all caused mine.

(Because I don't have a house, I can't be friends with those who do.) Aren't Blacks great folks?! Friends since birth; friends since elementary. Same neighborhood since elementary. I went to visit C_rm_n in college, Nic_y S. in college; visited S_lv_a in college; visited Va_es_a in college; visited Ch_nd_a I college. My girls just couldn't find it in their hearts to invite me to go out once they got home, married or not. I have to talk to someone. I have to hug someone. I'm embarrassed to call them my friends. (Former friends). (With the exception of maybe Ch_nd_a. She did invite me to lunch before she left.)

It's a feeling that you cannot describe unless you know Him as I do. An entire world can force you to be friends with the wicked and you can have peace in the midst. My doctor friend went to a school in an area that wasn't necessarily the best and a lot of her friends didn't fit into her 'doctor life'. But the world chose to force me to have delinquent friends so that they would think I was her. Now that I'm telling the truth. I'm slowly being murdered. I do not believe she is a ho either. It's not a measure of wit when your success is being controlled and sabotaged. I think that makes them, who are the controllers, the pathetic ones.

No I cannot handle jail. Not even if the cells are bars and not a door. I cannot ride in a 15 passenger van. I'm all my daughter has. They've supposedly replaced me with my grandson and her so called (former gang member, boyfriend). They want to kill me because they don't believe I'm a fit mother. I did everything I could to earn money legally. "We don't need to order her book". She's about to be dead. She just doesn't know it yet. (Now charge her with trespassing.) And invite her to church to sell her three books so we can say she's the Carrie girl. They want to quickly kill me before I write more books. I planned to write thousands of books. I never saw my life when I watched Sex in the City. I never used to watch the TV series.

Ghetto Language is So Different

Living in this ghetto at the bottom of the beltway, really has opened my eyes to so much. Just riding on the bus brings tears to my eyes. Everyone who left me outside, is delusional. They are all imaging that I am a single mother with four kids, on the bus.

This is what I hear around me: "Oh she closed." " Yeah, she a ho." "Bit_h." "Fu_k you." "Nigga." "She mus' not be walking." "Does it hurt, You're her?" "Cause you was open." I do not identify with this crazy talk. I'm not her or him or the fish or the dog, I'm just me.

The other day there was a man standing at the door of the CVS. He was saying, "Singles." I offered him some change. I thought he was asking for a dollar. Oh my God, he was selling single cigarettes.

All of the men walk around with alcohol in their hands. You very rarely see the few who don't, cause they stay inside.

All of those who read my books and believe I'm admitting that the characters are me, aren't really literate. It's slander!

Angela C. Williams

You Ho. I Love

Stop calling me a ho. I did not have a baby for companionship. I did not get pregnant before I was married. I didn't get married before I graduated from college.

I purposed my life to serve my daughter as unto God. I wanted her to have the best life she could have. I didn't want her in DC. I didn't want her in a shelter. I didn't want her around a lot of cursing, fighting, smoking and drinking. I did not want her in school in the District.

Things never work out for me because it always has to fit their next movie scene. It's deeply rooted sabotage.

Christians; What!

As I sat on the street many people who did not profess to be Christians showed a lot of compassion for my situation. After so many years, that compassion turned to cynicism.

But none the less, they were the ones who came through when I needed a place to rest for the night. Just a place to rest for the night. Unfortunately, the few who led me on, and I gave into emotionally/sexually, in what I believed was a relationship (several months or years we were together); negate all of the noble acts of those who were valiant in my time of need.

Blacks of all people, kicking folks when their down. What happened to loving like Jesus and WWJD. Where was the help from Christian women?

Then there were those who hid from me, at church. Those who talked a good game of Jesus and prayed like warriors but in the end, left you standing on the sidewalk, wondering when you would ever eat or sleep inside again.

I sat at my first vending table at Howard University this past Sunday and sold some of my books. Not many. But it's a start. As J Moss sang, they seemed to be feeling the move of the spirit. But how could that be. During this same moment, they were loudly, and clearly verbally harassing me as I sat peacefully at my table. They weren't sanding far from my table. (Just absolutely, nuts). Unfortunately, I have a court date at the end of the month that will seal my fate. I am claustrophobic and the citation I received for pan-handling can result in jail time for me. If I flee, I will receive a warrant. They did this on purpose so that I won't be able to have anything in my name. I won't be able to drive or have a bank account. If my case is not dismissed, I will never vote for another Black person in any election; (even if I would have been able to).

Jesus; Black's are stupid and trifling! Oh My God! I'm being set-up by millionaires, my family is mentally ill and ungodly and my friends are brainwashed, snooty whoremongers. **I do not deserve to go to jail. And I'm also claustrophobic. I would go to court if I would be guaranteed a year of house-arrest instead of jail.**

You're all mistaken about me-(This is expressed to the other races as well). I watched the movie *The Other Woman* 4 to 5 times before I saw it the way you see it because I know the truth. I would never string along 2 or three men at a time. I was not being a ho. And I do not have a dark side. I was hurt by 3 men on a job I had for 2 years. I was charged with trespassing or pan-handling so that I would run against a warrant and lose either my life and/or my life insurance money from my elderly father. Who's idea was it? Everybody conspired against me. It is the least that I can do to day to you DIE, while talking to myself indoors because of what you've done. I am not violent. You started killing me first. You killed my financial life, my social life to a certain extent, even my spiritual life out of my personal prayer closet. I was talking out loud to myself about sleeping with the president. That's what people do in their homes. They vent about there mean boss croaking or about their ex-wife failing at her career. That's normal. (Are they listening) I am not looking for a man. Especially not a married one. Do I sweat more than most women (Juwanna Mann or am I still single because I'm not moving)? God sees everything I do and He knows everything I'm thinking. I bought books that I'd written, to sell; not guns. I haven't done anything that causes for me to be arrested or put in jail. **I was literally forced to pan-handle by the entire world**. They think I'm acting when I show hurt. May Jesus forgive them and have mercy upon their souls. There is nothing I can say to a judge who's been brainwashed for over 20 years regarding my so called behavior. It's impossible to get a fair trial. My name has been dragged into every scenario on screen. I am being lied on. People don't smell me in public. I am not a ho now, nor did I used to be.

It's not the White people in court who have to judge me that concern me. It's the Black people who allowed this to happen in the first place. I should never have been forced to beg for income.

My Baby Grandson

He will never know how much I loved him. He will never know how much his mother tore my heart out. I wanted for her to succeed and I believe she is on her way. (And not because of the car my daughter bought). I sacrificed getting a job after she graduated from high-school because I wanted to make sure that he had someone watching him who truly loved him. He will never know how many people believed millions of lies about me. He will never know how much I sacrificed so that his mother would not have to live in a dirty, unsafe, inner-city shelter with dangerous street people. I wanted to cook for her. She had breakfast in the morning before school and she wore a clean uniform every day. He will never know how desperate everyone on this planet wants to make it seem as if I am the unlikable character in every movie. Research it. Pay close attention. I'm innocent. They want to murder me and blame me for missing airplanes and crashing trains. I have no phone most of the time, and no money. It's not my fault. I live my worst nightmare every day because of the lies on TV, on the radio and now out of the mouths of everyone who sees and hears the libel and slander! They ruined my life unjustly. Dustin is not the person they believe. My friends want me dead for mentioning their names in this book because they can't touch the writers and directors that hurt them, in Hollywood. I have a voice and somehow I am being heard by many. I suppose you believe I have a responsibility to watch what I say. Well, they have an awful large voice in Hollywood and they ever watch what they say.

I'm innocent and I'm telling the truth. I think the court is confused, the think I'm E. V. He's a cheating, lying, sex addict and poor excuse for a man. They thick my brother is my cousin. His mother is terrified of dogs (Disney Villains). He and I are being set-up, royally. It's inconceivable.

He will never know how many times a day I changed his paper so that he would not get diaper rash. He will never know how loyal I was to his grandfather. He will never know how much I loved the women who chose to not be my friend because of the rumors they believed. He will never know how scared I was on July 29th, 2015 because I now know that police believe that I was a loose slut. He will know just like I will, what my fate is. Since I can't get justice, I better find somewhere to hide. If the police understood what Hollywood was doing to me they wouldn't have given me that ticket. They would help me. Shooting me in the leg would get me in a hospital and out of a jail but I do not deserve that either. I do not deserve to be shot or charged with anything. I'm telling the truth. I'm being lied on by millions. I'm not a cheater or a ho.

My Only Daughter

I loved her. I'm glad that she is able to take care of herself. I'm glad that when I die, my father will still be here to help her. She does not hug me or say she loves me. I do not find it extraordinary that she is working and has an apartment. I expect that. I only hope that she continues to focus on school so that she will not have to break her back to work for the rest of her life. I pray that she does not get involved with any men romantically. I pray that she stays single but if she marries this K_lv_n guy, I hope he is not violent. I pray that they raise their child in the fear of the Lord.

If had the money I would have brought her flowers every day when we were homeless. You know what really hurts. An old white woman is still standing on the median pan-handling. She lives in Motel 6. The police don't bother her. Maybe if I was dirty and less attractive, I wouldn't be hassled. I'm a younger, thin, dark-skinned Black woman. I'm supposed to lay on my back for money. But the saddest part about this is that the ignorant Blacks on the bus, kept saying, yeah she's a ho, even knowing that I stood in 26 degree weather for money, for years, for my child to be away from them. I'm being punished for not selling sex. They could have given me house arrest for a year. Safeway could have dropped the charges. I'm a productive member of society whose child is a college student.

I think my daughter believes I was a ho. I guess it's all in how you look at things. Just a small group of the wrong friends in high-school and this is the out-come. It could have been much worse had she gone to school in DC. Maybe one day she will grow up to walk in the love of God. She'll learn that the truth that you hold inside, makes a world of difference. Because when she says something disrespectful; which isn't often, I know that's why it's being said. I can't work and she can. Everyone thinks I can't work because I used to be an easy slut and they believe people smelled me on my jobs. But I know the truth.

My Lovely Mother is Gone

I no longer think that my mother made a mistake with her children. I believe those who made the mistake are the ones who's children allowed this to happen to me and my daughter. I didn't want their husbands. I do not steal. They had more than enough room and food to help us for a long time. They are ashamed to call me their friend. (How can you be friends with someone like Angela-Why Did I Get Married?) I'm ashamed to call them, my friends.

My mother was the host to so many. She opened her home to our family. She was one of the kindest women I've ever known. I was doing everything that I could to bring honor to her even as she rests with God. All of her work, would not be for nothing. But Blacks were hell-bent on stopping me for reasons only The Devil himself will ever know. I had a plan. They sabotaged it before it had a chance to flourish. Blacks are not kind to each other at all. Look what you've done to her children. I probably could have gotten another job but my daughter had a baby. She needed me to watch my grandson. I should have had 25 strong years to work after getting him into daycare, which is just about to happen. My books sells are taking off, and now you want to end my life.

Angela C. Williams

I Miss My Brother

I do not know my brothers story completely but I have great memories of our lives together. He is definitely one of the reasons why I trusted men, as an evolving woman. I thought men were great. A healthy childhood is clearly very important. I only hope I see him again before they all kill me. I hope he has good news.

My Father Means Well

He is definitely the other reason why I trusted men as a young woman. He treated my mother well. They traveled the world. This should never have happened to me. He should have listened to me. He should have been sending me money without me asking. I'm not lazy. And I can keep a job. The sabotage is overwhelming. My need to be under a stable roof, was immediate. My daughter and myself. And a long time ago, my brother as well. I'm not sure of his situation now. I'm still in dier need of his help today.

Empty The Jails: Let's Start Over

All of the Blacks who couldn't get a fair trial years ago, are still in jail. I don't care if we let out 10 guilty people for every 1 innocent person. It would be well worth it. Keep the serial killer s behind bars.

It's all lies about me and my brother. The truth has been mangled and made into something horrible. I think those who are still here blaming me for the tower falling and planes being lost and trains and boats flipping over, are the ones who have the serious issues. Let's crucify somebody.

Who Is Messing Up The World?

Is it you? Are you messing up the world? Ask yourself. Are you messing up yourself? Are you trying hard to mess up someone else's life? Are you trying to keep someone from prospering?

Do you think a woman who gives her husband permission to go out and sleep with other unsuspecting woman, is messing up the world?

Do you think that a man who is very attractive and fit, who marries a woman who is obese and unattractive to many, with an attitude problem; because he has a warrant and needs someone keep him, is messing up the world?

Do you think that a millionaire who distorts a working person's personal information and aires it incorrectly on TV and in film is messing up the world?

Do you think ha a judge who gives 90 days in jail instead of 1 year of house arrest, to a pan-handler; is messing up the world?

Do you think a woman who marries a man who is rebounded from a failed marriage that happened before he finished college, is messing up the world by marrying him again before he re-enters college and gets his degree?

Do you think that a woman who speaks through a television set (not during a show) and says "I told you I could ruin you" to a woman who pan-handled to keep her daughter out of inner city shelters, and is watching her grandson for free while writing books to earn money; is messing up the world by ensuring that this college educated, quiet, private, claustrophobic woman gets a charge and is potentially jailed? (Because I gave some more information to clear me and my brother from taking the fall for her and a lot of other people, in a particular movie?) I know this can't be about me taking someone's husband; I'm single and I'm never looking for a man.

Angela C. Williams

You can't tell me that novels that are written with common situations from everyday people haven't been inspired in some shape or form, from someone's personal life. I choose not to write books like that. I leave you to wonder nothing and I don't change names and pretend its fiction; if I'm speaking of someone real. And you need not worry about rather or not me or them, slept with a man unless he's your husband and you had no idea. In which case, we probably were being lied to as well.

Do you think that a working woman educating herself, whose body calls for sex and she keeps the same partner for 10 years because she loves him, knowing she will never marry him, is messing up the world?

Do you think those who bullied in elementary and are still bullying on their jobs, are messing up the world?

Are parents who won't let their children live with them because they don't have a job, messing up the world? What if the kid is actively looking for work? Some people have warrants because they break the law while living with their parents. Some people have warrants because they were left homeless by their parents and family. Their situations are probably not the same. There are bad kids and there are bad parents.

Do you think that a woman who is left outside by every person in the human race, who sleeps with a man (after however long), who is supposedly single and riding her to her destinations all over town. Introduces her to his family and moves her in with his sister or moves in with her (wherever), but he is ultimately lying; is messing up the world? (Although you wanted it to be the case, the author of this book never had sex for shelter or money or for a ride).Do you think of me when you watch Baggage Claim? Why?

I danced like that with a man who took me in from the Post office or siting at the laundromat; from the heat. I slept in his bed, he slept on the sofa but He never touched my body other than a hug –(no stethoscope). I never leaned on anyone's shoulder for comfort. (Now I don't want a man and the reason is 'cause I'm hurt; I don't think so.) They're lying in the movies. I believe I'm a great person and always have felt that way about myself.

For people who went to such expensive, well-known; colleges, those in the MD/DC/VA area sure seem perplexed and misled.

I should have received a written pardon form someone. I'm a productive citizen and I'm not ho. I didn't used to be a ho either. I'm not ghetto and I don't have sex anywhere. I am being set-up and sabotaged. (My grandson hugs me now. Soon he'll be able to talk).

Please Don't Look For Me

So you can shoot me in my leg (smiles). Why do you want to kill me? Is it ok for a cop to give a ticket to someone so that they can put them in a position where shooting them seems proper because the cop didn't like a comment written about bad cops, in one of those person's books?

They Can't Possibly Have Female Relatives

I don't know what our Black men are thinking sometimes. They really think that there are women who don't want and/or don't deserve to have a committed, healthy eventful relationship. I guess they must not have had decent relationships with their moms or aunt's or grandma's. And they definitely can't have daughters of their own.

You can treat a woman kindly without spending money at the movies etc. But if that is desired than there will be a problem.

You Believe It's About Me, But It's Not

I don't know how to feel about the fact that you will always think about me when you watch movies, even when I'm gone. The thoughts are warped, wrong and demonic but you will be thinking about me.

It hurts more than you will ever know to watch a movie and enjoy it 3 times, only to watch it again and see that they are attempting to convince the world that you (me), are a cheater, liar, thief or violent vengeful slut. People who don't even know me, hate me already.

See they all believe that I'm the one in the library knocking over stuff while having sex. I've never had that kind of sex. Never had sex in a library but some of the other information I told to guys I've dated; like my husband running into the court room yelling, why. He didn't want a divorce. So when they see the movie they will think about me and associate all of it's non-sense with me. Those who don't understand how this keeps me from working, must be slow.

I think they don't think I matter because I "wasted" my degree. (Chocolate, wasted)-*Grown-ups.* They all know that I haven't had sex since my grandson was born over 16-17 months ago and they are trying to get me to get pregnant so that I will be more comfortable in jail I suppose. See they all believe that I'm the one in the library knocking over stuff while having sex. I've never had that kind of sex. Never had sex in a library but some of the other information I told to guys I've dated; like my husband running into the court room yelling, why. He didn't want a divorce. So when they see the movie they will think about me and associate all of it's non-sense with me. I think they don't think I matter because I "wasted" my degree. (Chocolate, wasted)-*Grown-ups.* They all know that I haven't had sex since my grandson was born over 16-17 months ago and they are trying to get me to get pregnant so that I will be more comfortable in jail I suppose.

Attorneys and Politicians

All of these Black Attorney's and Politicians who are making all of this money and making all of these decisions, seemed to have forgotten about those locked up. There are too many innocent people in jail. Too many people who could have been punished in other humane ways. Laws need to be changed. That needs to be our focus. If they have house arrest or community service, we can still reach them. All of the Blacks who didn't have a fair trial. All of the non-violent crimes that happened by accident or set-ups. Because It's inconclusive, they should not be locked in a cell. Jesus!

My Heart Is Right and It Always Has Been

I can still smile at my grandson and pray for my daughter, knowing that everyone on this planet is currently planning my unjustified murder. The people in power used to uneducated people to hurt me and sabotage my life while the 'smart' people sat and watched it happen.

Whether or not there was an insurance plan for me, I wanted to be with my dad. Maybe I don't know him like I thought I did.

My Death Poem to Me

When I die, I know I'll hear the voice of my savior. And I'll see my mom again.
I pray that the man appointed to judge me and place me in a cell, knows life's answers well.
The man who had the power to free me as he should, sat and watched me fall.
Taking away my air-supply hardly seems befitting for a pan-handling charge.
I cannot go before the judge, cause Black people set me up.

(Not always begging) Six years we thrived and life began to get better. They did not want me to pan-handle, but favor must have said let her.

Then the last time I stood outside to get my prescription, I got a charge that ended my life. Those in power, did it on purpose. Those in wonderland caused it.

I realize I never had a friend in the world. Not a boy, not a girl.

My Large Extended Family Knew Jesus

Did they ever know His children. Jesus wants us to love one-another. You left me to die... I love my brother...I loved my mother and she knew it...I love my father, even though I do not understand his ways...

Do you remember the Christmas card I gave you in 2001? The poem. When did you stop loving me?

Why did you not offer me shelter until I had steady income?

A Community That Wants Me To go To Jail For Pan-handling

They made sure to tell me as I sat on the metro bus: what to expect on the bus, headed to jail. They told me what to eat and told me that I will survive. Doesn't that just disgust you. Why couldn't I just have a place to live and not be harassed on the 4 jobs I acquired.

I Can't Even Get a Fair Trial

Because of the lies of the writers in Hollywood and because I have no friends or family and no one to hug or talk to.

Hollywood can make movies shooting pastors when you're angry, blowing up judges when they answer the phone and robbing banks when you don't have enough money, but I can't even vent in my own daughters apartment about being sabotaged.

Pay very close attention to this part. It's the reason why I know I wouldn't get a fair trial anywhere on this planet. I'll start by saying that every person believes that my hygiene is the reason why I'm single. I don't change my pad enough and I'm leaking. They believe that I didn't have a strong enough deodorant. Somehow there was a forum for all of those in an intimate situation with me to tell the"truth". I smelled like outside, because of the dress that I wore. It absorbed outside scents. But I was smelled; (sniffed). Someone is assigned to sniff me wherever I go; work, social event; to see if I smell. I was sniffed at the Howard event even before I went into the restroom to powder up after walking from the bus stop for 10 minutes to get to the building. My deodorant is Clinical. My pad is fine. Now I'm a liar, because I really do smell and I must have smelled in every intimate situation; and on my jobs. (The event was not sponsored by Howard University). I'm not mad at her. I thank her for even inviting me. It was the first time that any Christian woman had found a way for me to earn money in a Christian environment. Judges and police believe I sell or sold sex. Everyone hates me for some reason.

God's Timing is So Far Beyond Us All

It's not for you to decide when God wants to use someone and let their talents show. My books were written when God wanted them to be written. Not when Carrie wrote hers. But I guess you all win. You sabotaged my life and now it will be very hard to prosper. I'm sure Satan is very proud.

Angela C. Williams

www.ingramcontent.com/pod-product-compliance
Lightning Source LLC
Chambersburg PA
CBHW030547290526
45786CB00004B/1909